# My First Shark Book

By Carrie Casey

Thank you so much for purchasing this book! I had so much fun creating this book for you to enjoy. I trust you will have as much fun reading it as I did creating it.

If you like this book, I'd be most grateful if you'd help me out by taking a few moments and leaving a review on Amazon. Thank you so much!

As a FREE BONUS for purchasing this eBook, for a limited time, we'd like to gift you a shark coloring packet for you and your loved ones to add your own color and creativity to. Go to https://carrieecasey.clickfunnels.com/sharkbook to get your packet.

Peace, love, and splashes,
Carrie Casey

Published by CEY Press
821 Grand Ave, Suite 119
Pflugerville, TX 78660

Copyright © 2021 by Carrie Casey
My First Shark Book: A Rhyming Animal Book for Young Children

All rights reserved. No part of this publication may be reproduced, distributed, or transmitted in any form or by any means, including photocopying, recording, or other electronic or mechanical methods, without the prior written permission of the publisher.

ISBN: 978-1-954885-08-0

Text copyright © 2021 by Carrie Casey
Illustrations provided by George Desipris, Gerald Schombs, Ben Phillips, Jakob Owens, Mile Ribeiro, Leonardo Lamas, Nariman Mesharrafa, & Fran Jesus Navarro Hernandez

# My First Shark Book

By Carrie Casey

SHARKS SLIDE SWIFTLY THROUGH THE SEAS.

GREAT WHITE WHO RULES THE OCEAN DEEP, WHAT SECRETS DO THOSE SHARP TEETH KEEP?

THIS SHARK SWIMS IN SEAS SO DARK.

WHALE SHARKS WILL NOT FLEE FROM YOU. THEY ARE SO BIG THAT THEY DO NOT HAVE TO.

IT SHOULD BE KNOWN THAT MANY SHARKS DO NOT LIKE TO BE ALONE.

HAVE YOU EVER THOUGHT THAT A SHARK WOULD HAVE MORE THAN ONE SPOT? THIS ONE HAS A LOT.

THESE TEETH SEIZE THEIR FOOD AS THEY SWIM ACROSS THE SEAS.

THIS ANGEL SHARK DOES NOT MAKE A SOUND AS SHE LIES ON THE GROUND.

BABY SHARK HIDES
AS HE GLIDES.

SMILING SHARK SWIMS FROM LIGHT TO DARK.

SOMETIMES THEY JUST WANT TO HAVE FUN IN THE SUN.

THIS LEMON SHARK SWIMS ABOVE THE SEAGRASS.

AND THIS LEOPARD SHARK GIVES THE FISH A PASS.

SOME HAVE SLIM FACES.

# SOME HAVE WIDE FACES.

SWIFT SHARKS SLIP AND SLIDE THEIR WAY THROUGH SEAS ALONE OR IN GROUPS AND ALWAYS POWERFULLY.

Thank you so much for purchasing this book! We had so much fun creating this book for you to enjoy. We trust you will have as much fun reading it as we did creating it.

We enjoy making basic science content accessible to young children. The more we can feed the love of the natural world, the more they will soak up science knowledge.

If you like this book, we'd be most grateful if you'd help us out by taking a few moments and leaving us a review on Amazon. Thank you so much!

As a FREE BONUS for purchasing this eBook, for a limited time, we'd like to gift you a shark coloring pack for you and your loved ones to add your own color and creativity to. Just go to https://carrieecasey.clickfunnels.com/sharkbook to get your packet.

Peace, love, and splashes,
Carrie Casey

Carrie Casey is a wife of one, mom of two young adults, entrepreneur, businesswoman poet whose life's work is about spreading joy through education.

At the age of 3, she decided that she would have a center when she grew up. By 23 She had achieved her dream. She has owned three childcare centers in the Austin, Texas area. Through a series of unusual circumstances, she spent several years in real estate development, before returning to educational program support.

When she is not mentoring directors, teachers, and parents, Carrie can be found wandering through nature, reading, traveling theworld, and/or enjoying pastries; she currently resides in a city she loves, most likely multitasking.

Keep in touch with Carrie via the web:
Website: https://www.texasdirector.com/
Facebook: http://www.facebook.com/texasdirector
Podcast: https://colorfulclipboard.buzzsprout.com/